2025

COSTA RICA

TRAVEL GUIDE

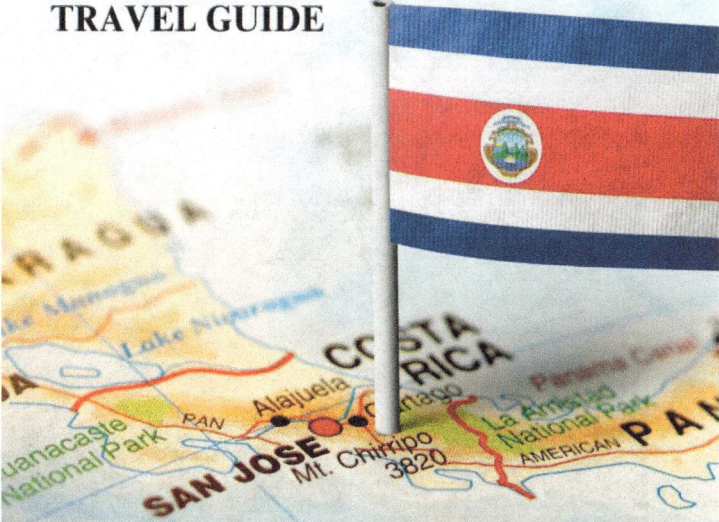

Discover Hidden Gems, Must-See Landmarks, and Eco-Friendly Adventures with Step-by-Step Itineraries, Maps, and Local Secrets for a Captivating Experience.

by_Stanley Moreland

Table of Contents

Welcome to Costa Rica

Adventurers, nature lovers, and those seeking the ideal getaway will find Costa Rica, a sliver of paradise nestled between the Pacific and Caribbean Seas, to be ideal. This tiny Central American nation delivers enormous experiences with its towering volcanoes, immaculate beaches, lush rainforests, and some of the world's happiest people. Costa Rica encourages you to slow down, re-establish a connection with nature, and experience its renowned "Pura Vida" way of life, whether you're ziplining through the canopy, seeing sloths in the wild, or enjoying a freshly made cup of local coffee.

Why Visit Costa Rica in 2025?

2025 is the ideal year to travel to Costa Rica if you've been looking for the ideal time to go. With new conservation initiatives, more access to national parks, and environmentally friendly travel experiences, the nation remains at the forefront of ecotourism. New boutique hotels and eco-lodges provide visitors with a cozy yet genuine way to take in the natural splendor of the nation, while recent infrastructure improvements make traveling easier than ever. With an expanding array of festivals, cultural events, and new adventure excursions, Costa Rica is sure to create experiences that will last a lifetime.

.

About This Guide

This guide is your go-to resource for organizing a smooth, enjoyable, and profoundly enlightening vacation—it's more than just a list of sights to visit and activities. Whether you're an experienced traveler or a first-time visitor, we've created this guide to help you discover the best of Costa Rica, complete with expert advice, comprehensive itineraries, and local secrets. This guide will help you feel like an experienced tourist from the time you arrive, covering everything from using public transportation to locating the tastiest street cuisine.

Pura Vida: The Costa Rican Lifestyle

The word "Pura Vida" is used everywhere in Costa Rica, from warm welcomes to farewells, and even in response to the question, "How are you?" But Pura Vida is more than just a collection of words; it's a way of life. Its meaning, "pure life," captures the nation's profound love of contentment, simplicity, and a close relationship with the natural world. It serves as a reminder to enjoy the present, let go of needless worry, and embrace joy. You will witness Pura Vida in action as you travel across Costa Rica—in the kind smiles of the people, the leisurely pace of life, and the efforts made to preserve the environment. You may find yourself bringing a little Pura Vida home with you when your trip is over.

Planning Your Trip

A vacation to Costa Rica is an experience of a lifetime, and it may run as smoothly as the nation's well-known golden beaches provided it is planned properly. Your go-to resource for creating a memorable, stress-free trip is this chapter. We can help you with everything from choosing when to travel to figuring out how to get about. Let's get started!

Best Time to Visit: Dry vs. Rainy Seasons

Two words best describe Costa Rica's climate: dry and wet. The ideal time to visit depends on the type of experience you're seeking because every season offers a different viewpoint on the nation's natural splendor.

From December to April, the dry season:

This is Costa Rica's peak season, which is referred to locally as "verano" (summer). Anticipate bright sky, dry roads, and perfect weather for hiking, beach visits, and national park exploration. But since it's also the busiest season, make reservations for lodging and activities well in advance.

Rainy Season (May to November):

Also termed "invierno" (winter), this is Costa Rica's green season. Afternoon showers are typical but bring out the lush, vivid beauty of the rainforests. It's the ideal time of year for amazing waterfalls, cheaper prices, and more tranquil hikes. While September and October are perfect for visiting the Caribbean side, they might be especially rainy on the Pacific coast.

Pro Tip: For a balance between good weather and fewer crowds, consider visiting in late November or early December before the holiday rush.

Entry Requirements & Travel Documents

It's easy to travel to Costa Rica, but it's crucial to have your documentation in order:

- Passport: Verify that it will still be valid six months after the dates of your travel.
- Visa: For visits of up to 90 days, the majority of visitors from North America, Europe, and many other nations do not require a visa. Before you go, confirm the requirements of your country.
- Return Ticket: Costa Rican immigration may ask for proof of a return or forward ticket.
- Vaccinations: While not required, it's a good idea to keep up with recommended vaccinations. A yellow fever vaccination certificate is necessary if you are coming from a nation where there is a danger of contracting the disease.

Pro Tip: Make digital and physical copies of your important documents. Email a set to yourself for easy access.

Packing Essentials for Every Traveler

A combination of adventure basics and tropical-ready gear is needed when packing for Costa Rica:

Dressing:

- Breathable, lightweight clothing for hot weather.
- A waterproof jacket or poncho for unexpected downpours.
- Sturdy sandals or hiking shoes for path exploration.
- Quick-dry towels and swimwear.
- A hat and sunglasses to protect against the sun. Equipment: Binoculars for observing wildlife.
- A reusable water bottle (filtered water is available at many hotels).

- A waterproof bag or case for electronics.

- Insect repellant and sunscreen.

Other Essentials:

- Medications and a basic first-aid kit.
- Plug adapters if needed (Costa Rica uses 120V and standard U.S. outlets).
- A small backpack for day trips.

Pro Tip: Pack light! Many domestic flights and shuttles have strict luggage limits.

Health & Safety Tips

Costa Rica is a safe place, however taking precautions guarantees your trip stays trouble-free:

- Healthcare: Costa Rica has outstanding healthcare services in urban areas. It is strongly advised to purchase travel insurance.
- Water: In most places, tap water is safe to drink, but in rural regions, use bottled or filtered water instead.
- Wildlife: Respect animals from a distance because some may be poisonous or disease-carrying.
- Beach Safety: Swim only in approved locations and watch out for rip currents.
- Personal Safety: Keep your possessions safe, especially in crowded places, as petty theft can happen.

Pro Tip: Get the emergency contact information for the "Embassy of your country in Costa Rica" here.

Budgeting for Your Costa Rican Adventure

Costa Rica can be as opulent or as inexpensive as you want it to be:

- Lodging options range from luxurious resorts ($200+/night) to hostels ($10–$25/night).
- Meals: While gourmet dining might cost over $30, local sodas (little restaurants) serve meals for $5 to $10.
- Activities: Entrance fees to national parks range from $10 to $20, while guided excursions cost between $50 and $100.
- Transportation: Car rentals start at $30 per day, but public buses are inexpensive ($1 to $15).

Pro Tip: Major credit cards are frequently accepted, but for little transactions, always have some cash on hand in colones (local currency).

Navigating Transportation: Flights, Cars, Buses & Boats

Traveling throughout Costa Rica is a component of the adventure:

- Flights: Domestic travel is swift and picturesque. The primary carriers are Nature Air and Sansa.

- Renting a car is a great way to see places that are less traveled. If you intend to travel to rural or mountainous areas, get a 4x4.

- Buses: Reasonably priced and dependable for low-budget vacationers. TicaBus and other long-distance buses are pleasant for traveling between cities.

- Boats: A must for traveling across the Gulf of Nicoya or to locations like Tortuguero.

- Rideshares & Taxis: While Uber and other apps are available in major cities, red taxis are the official mode of transportation.

Pro Tip: Use Waze, the preferred navigation app in Costa Rica, as it's more accurate than Google Maps for local roads.

Top Destinations in Costa Rica

Costa Rica is a small country with a vast array of experiences packed into its borders. From vibrant cities to pristine beaches, lush rainforests, and towering mountains, there's something for every kind of traveler. This chapter breaks down the country's most iconic and under-the-radar destinations, giving you the latest insights to craft a memorable trip. Despite its tiny size, Costa Rica offers a wide range of experiences. Every type of traveler can find something they enjoy, from energetic cities to immaculate beaches, verdant rainforests, and majestic mountains. This chapter provides you with the most recent information to help you plan an unforgettable vacation by breaking down the nation's most famous and lesser-known locations.

San José and the Central Valley

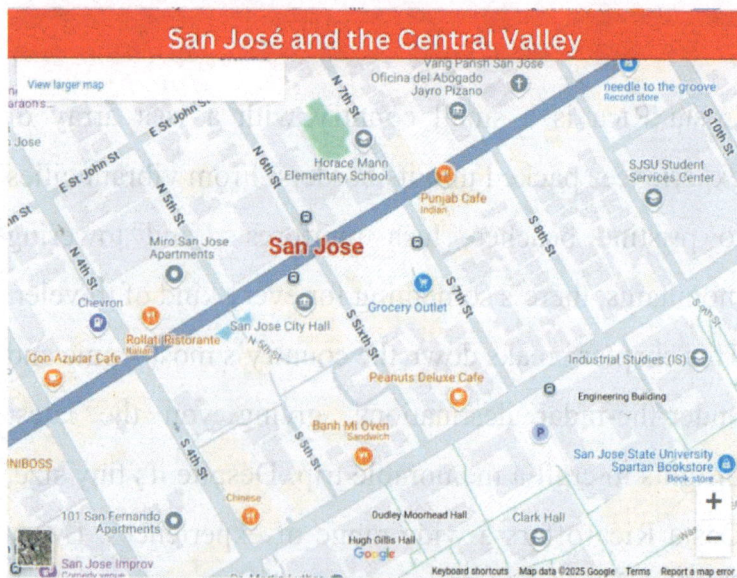

San José and the Central Valley

SCAN THE QR CODE

STEPS:

- **Open your smartphone's camera app or a QR code scanning app.**
- **Point the camera steadily at the QR code.**
- **Wait for a notification or link to appear.**
- **Tap the link to access the content.**

Cultural Landmarks & Urban Life

Costa Rica's bustling capital, San José, is more than just a gateway—it's a treasure trove of culture and history. Set in the Central Valley and surrounded by coffee plantations, it's a great place to explore museums, local markets, and the lively Tico urban vibe.

- National Theater: A stunning 19th-century architectural gem offering guided tours and performances.
- Museums: Don't miss the Pre-Columbian Gold Museum and National Museum, which delve into Costa Rica's rich history and culture.
- Local Markets: Mercado Central is perfect for sampling traditional dishes like casados or buying artisan souvenirs.
- Nearby Excursions: Visit Poás Volcano National Park for a dramatic crater view or La Paz Waterfall Gardens to experience stunning cascades and wildlife exhibits.

Pro Tip: San José is the country's transport hub, so plan your stay here strategically to access nearby attractions.

The Pacific Coast

The Pacific Coast

SCAN THE QR CODE

STEPS:
- Open your smartphone's camera app or a QR code scanning app.
- Point the camera steadily at the QR code.
- Wait for a notification or link to appear.
- Tap the link to access the content.

The Pacific coast of Costa Rica is a haven for surfers, beachcombers, and adventurers. It offers a variety of landscapes and activities and stretches from Guanacaste to the Osa Peninsula.

- Guanacaste: Surfing hotspots and beach resorts. Some of Costa Rica's most stunning beaches may be found on Guanacaste, also referred to as the "Gold Coast."
- Tamando: A vibrant surf town with excellent food options, a vibrant nightlife, and world-class waves.
- Playa Flamingo: A more sedate option with luxurious resorts and immaculate beaches.
- Papagayo Peninsula: The pinnacle of luxury, featuring eco-friendly architecture and exclusive resorts.
- Rincón de la Vieja National Park: Discover hot springs, waterfalls, and volcanic scenery.

- Nicoya Peninsula: Yoga, relaxation, and well-being. The relaxed atmosphere and wellness retreats of the Nicoya Peninsula are well-known.

Santa Teresa: A bohemian beach town perfect for surfing and yoga.

- Montezuma: With access to the Montezuma Waterfalls, Montezuma is a charming and artistic city.
- Blue Zone Discovery: Learn about the region's long-lived residents and healthy lifestyle.
- Santa Teresa is a free-spirited coastal town that's ideal for yoga and surfing.
- Montezuma: This quaint and creative city is home to the Montezuma Waterfalls.
- Blue Zone Discovery: Discover the long lifespan and healthy lifestyle of the area's inhabitants.
- Manuel Antonio & Jaco Adventures, Central Pacific. This area blends coastal bliss with rainforest activities.

- Manuel Antonio National Park: Hike trails that lead to remote beaches and see monkeys, sloths, and exotic birds.

- San José: An energetic town renowned for its thriving nightlife and surf culture.

- Carara National Park: A birdwatcher's haven, home to scarlet macaws and crocodiles.

- South Pacific: The Wild Osa Peninsula. The Osa Peninsula is a must-see for eco-tourists and is frequently referred to as the most ecologically dense location on Earth.

- Trek through a pristine rainforest teeming with wildlife in Corcovado National Park.

- Drake Bay: A secluded location for diving, snorkeling, and whale watching.

- Golfe Dulce: One of the world's few tropical fjords, perfect for kayaking and paddle boarding

.

The Caribbean Coast

The Caribbean Coast

SCAN THE QR CODE

STEPS:
- Open your smartphone's camera app or a QR code scanning app.
- Point the camera steadily at the QR code.
- Wait for a notification or link to appear.
- Tap the link to access the content.

Afro-Caribbean culture, verdant rainforests, and serene beaches are all mixed together in Costa Rica's Caribbean region.

- Puerto Viejo: Rainforests and Afro-Caribbean Feelings.
  This lively town is well-known for its amazing cuisine, relaxed atmosphere, and reggae music.
- Cahuita National Park: Take leisurely walks along the coast and snorkel among coral reefs.
- Gandoca-Manzanillo Wildlife Refuge: A remote location for seeing uncommon animals.
- Local Cuisine: Savor rice and beans cooked in coconut milk, among other Caribbean delicacies.

Turtle nesting and jungle canals in Tortuguero. The only ways to get to Tortuguero, frequently called the "Amazon of Costa Rica," are by boat or flight.

- Canal Tours: Cruise along waterways in the jungle that are filled with caimans, birds, and monkeys.

- Sea Turtles: See sea turtles nesting on the beach from July to October.

Northern Highlands

Northern Highlands

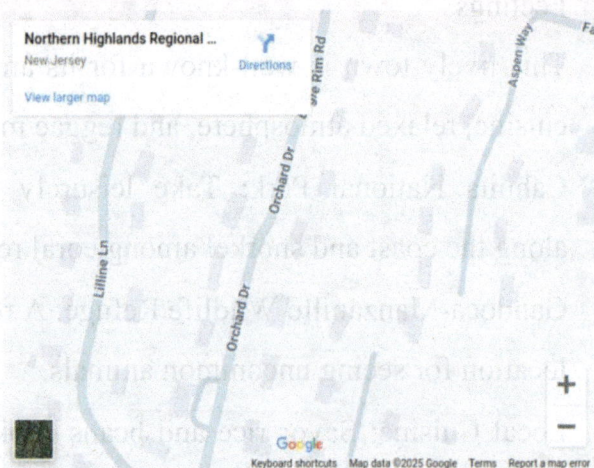

Northern Highlands Regional ...
New Jersey
Directions
View larger map

Google
Keyboard shortcuts Map data ©2025 Google Terms Report a map error

SCAN THE QR CODE

STEPS:
- Open your smartphone's camera app or a QR code scanning app.
- Point the camera steadily at the QR code.
- Wait for a notification or link to appear.
- Tap the link to access the content.

The highlands provide breathtaking scenery, leisure, and adventure.

La Fortuna and the Arenal Volcano: Adventure & Hot Springs.

The magnificent Arenal Volcano serves as a playground for both thrill-seekers and those who like to unwind.

- o Adventure Sports: Try white-water rafting, canyoning, or ziplining.
- o Hot Springs: Unwind in thermal pools at EcoTermales or Tabacón resorts.
- o Arena Lake: A popular location for stand-up paddleboarding, kayaking, and fishing.

Monteverde: Conservation and Cloud Forests.
Monteverde is a well-known site for ecotourism.

- o Monteverde Cloud Forest Reserve: Take a suspension bridge stroll among hazy treetops.
- o Night Tours: Go on guided night walks to see nocturnal creatures.

- o Coffee Tours: Discover how local farms produce coffee in Costa Rica.

Southern Highlands

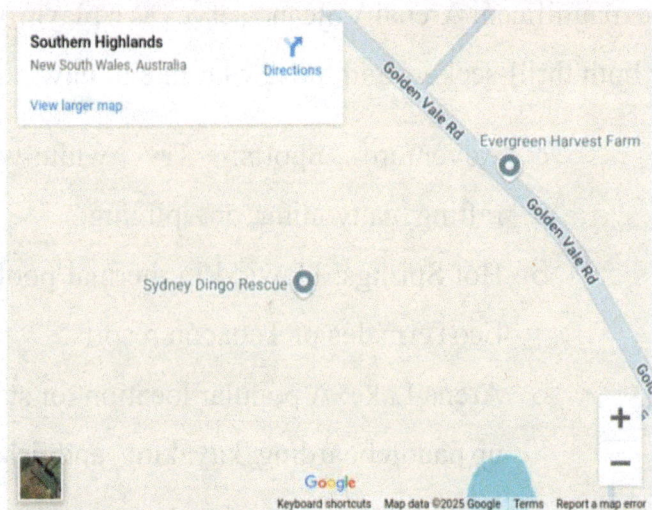

Southern Highlands

SCAN THE QR CODE

STEPS:

- Open your smartphone's camera app or a QR code scanning app.
- Point the camera steadily at the QR code.
- Wait for a notification or link to appear.
- Tap the link to access the content.

There are fantastic hiking options and milder temps in this less-traveled area.

Hiking the Highest Peak in Costa Rica: Cerro Chirripó.

The highest point in Costa Rica is Cerro Chirripó, which stands at 3,821 meters (12,536 feet).

- Chirripó National Park: Trek through a variety of environments, including páramo (tundra-like) landscapes and rainforests.
  - Summit Views: On clear days, you can see the Pacific and Caribbean Seas.
  - San Gerardo de Rivas: A quaint base town with a unique local character and hot springs.

Wildlife & Nature Wonders

With an astounding 6% of the globe's total biodiversity contained inside 0.03% of the planet's landmass, Costa Rica is among the most biodiverse nations on the planet. With innumerable chances to see uncommon creatures, investigate virgin ecosystems, and take in the splendor of its surroundings, this natural wonderland is a sanctuary for nature lovers.

An Overview of Costa Rica's Biodiversity With more than 500,000 different plant and animal species, Costa Rica boasts unparalleled biodiversity. With eight ecological reserves, 19 animal refuges, and 29 national parks, there are plenty of protected locations to explore.

- Ecosystems: A remarkable range of life is supported by the diversity of habitats, which include mangroves, cloud forests, coral reefs, and volcanoes.

Highlights of the Wildlife:

- Mammals: Sloths, jaguars, and howler monkeys; Birds: More than 900 species, including the magnificent quetzal and scarlet macaw;
- Reptiles and Amphibians: Poison dart frogs, sea turtles, and crocodiles;

Fun Fact: Due to Costa Rica's dedication to conservation, nearly 30% of its land is protected;

Best National Parks to Visit Costa Rica's national parks are the crown jewels of its biodiversity.

Here are some places to visit for life-changing experiences:

- Corcovado National Park (Osa Peninsula) Corcovado is a must-visit for serious wildlife enthusiasts; Highlights: See all four species of Costa Rican monkeys, tapirs, scarlet macaws, and jaguars.

- Activities include overnight stays at ranger stations, guided walks, and birdwatching.

Pro Tip: For simpler trails and greater views of the wildlife, go between December and April, when it's dry.

Caribbean Coast Tortuguero National Park Tortuguero, a network of rainforest waterways brimming with life, is known as the "Amazon of Costa Rica."

- Activities include canoe tours, nighttime turtle walks, and jungle hikes. Highlights include seeing green sea turtles nesting (July–October) and gliding through canals to see manatees, caimans, and toucans.

Pro Tip: To see the most active wildlife, choose an early morning canal cruise.

Central Valley's Poás Volcano National Park
Poás boasts striking scenery and is home to one of the
world's largest active volcano craters.

- Highlights: Explore dwarf cloud forests and gaze
  into the blue sulfuric crater lake.
- Activities: Observing volcanoes and trekking
  scenic trails.

Pro Tip: Get there early because by mid-morning, the
crater is frequently hidden by clouds.

National Park Marino Ballena (South Pacific Coast)

This park is a haven for marine life and is well-known
for its "Whale Tail" sandbar formation.

- Highlights: coral reefs, dolphins, and humpback
  whale migrations (July–October, December–
  March).

- Activities include snorkeling, whale watching excursions, and beach exploration.

Pro Tip: Take a stroll around the Whale Tail formation when it's low tide.

Northern Highlands' Monteverde Cloud Forest Reserve

A haven for eco-tourists, Monteverde is a mysterious forest covered in mist.

- Activities include guided hikes, canopy tours, and night safaris. Highlights include seeing vibrant quetzals, hiking suspension bridges, and seeing a variety of plant life, such as orchids and bromeliads.

Pro Tip: Wear sturdy shoes and a rain jacket—it's called a cloud forest for a reason!

Birdwatching and Wildlife Spotting Tips

Although Costa Rica is a haven for birdwatchers, even non-birdwatchers find the country's diverse fauna to be fascinating.

- Best Times for Wildlife: Peak activity occurs in the early morning and late afternoon.
  - Items to Bring: a field guide for wildlife and birds, binoculars, and a decent camera.
- Patience is essential: Keep quiet and let nature to speak for itself.

Monteverde, Tortuguero, and Carara National Park are the best places to go bird watching.

- Guides to Wildlife: Your experience can be substantially improved by hiring an experienced guide.

Marine Life: Whale Watching, Snorkeling, and Diving

The diversity of Costa Rica's terrestrial and marine ecosystems is equal. There are amazing chances to explore beneath the waters on both coasts. One of the rare locations where you may witness humpback whales from both the Northern and Southern Hemispheres is Costa Rica.

The Gulf of Papagayo, Drake Bay, and Marino Ballena National Park are the best places to visit. The seasons are July through October and December through March.

Diving and Snorkeling

Top Locations:

The Caño Island Biological Reserve is home to stunning coral reefs and a wealth of marine life, such as turtles, rays, and sharks.

- Located along the Caribbean coast, the Gandoca-Manzanillo Wildlife Refuge is a hidden gem for snorkeling.
- Experiences with manta rays and whale sharks are popular in the Catalina Islands.

Tips: Bring reef-safe sunscreen to protect marine ecosystems and consider taking a guided tour to access the best underwater spots.

Adventures & Activities

From heart-pounding excitement to tranquil getaways, Costa Rica is an adventurer's paradise. This nation offers unique experiences for every visitor, whether they include riding waves, basking in natural hot springs, or soaring through rainforests.

Adventure Seekers: Canyoning, Rafting, and Ziplining

Experience the essence of Costa Rica by flying over lush rainforests on top-notch zipline courses.

Top Sites: • Monteverde: The site of Central America's longest zipline and the well-known Selvatura Park.

- Arenal: Ziplining above the Arenal Volcano is available at Sky Adventures.
- Tamando: Take advantage of canopy tours and enjoy views of the coastline.

Pro Tip: Choose early morning slots to avoid crowds and enjoy cooler weather.

Whitewater Rafting

Some of the world's greatest rafting experiences may be found on Costa Rica's rivers.

Top Rivers: One of the most picturesque rivers is the Pacuare, which has Class III–IV rapids and waterfalls.

- Savegre River: With Class II–III rapids and verdant surroundings, this river is perfect for families. This river is perfect for beginners because it has Class II–III rapids.
- For larger water levels and more powerful rapids, the rainy season, which runs from May to November, is the best time of year.

Canyoning

For a thrilling adventure, descend among gorges and waterfalls.

- Top Attractions: • Arena: Pure Trek Canyoning offers rappelling down waterfalls.
- Manuel Antonio: Incorporate exhilarating canyoning experiences with rainforest walks.

Pro Tip: Put on clothes that dry quickly and sturdy shoes with good traction.

Surfing Costa Rica: Best Beaches for Beginners and Pros

Costa Rica is a global surfing hotspot with consistent waves and stunning beaches for every skill level.

Best Beaches for Beginners

- Tamarindo (Pacific Coast): Known as "Surf City," Tamarindo offers gentle waves and plenty of surf schools.
- Playa Samara: Calm waters and a laid-back vibe make this perfect for first-timers.
- Puerto Viejo (Caribbean Coast): Playa Cocles has manageable waves and surf rentals nearby.

Best Beaches for Pros

- Playa Hermosa (Central Pacific): Powerful waves make it a favorite for advanced surfers.

- Witches' Rock (Guanacaste): Legendary for its long barrels, accessible via boat.
- Pavones (South Pacific): Home to one of the longest left-hand breaks in the world.

Pro Tip: The dry season (December to April) offers consistent surf conditions on the Pacific coast, while the Caribbean coast shines from November to February

Hiking Trails for All Levels

Costa Rica's diverse terrain means there's a trail for everyone, from leisurely walks to challenging treks.

Beginner-Friendly Trails

- La Fortuna Waterfall (Arenal): A short hike with a stunning 200-foot waterfall at the end.
- Hanging Bridges (Monteverde): A relaxed walk through the canopy with incredible views.

Intermediate Trails

- Rincón de la Vieja National Park: Explore bubbling mud pots, waterfalls, and volcanic landscapes.
- Manuel Antonio National Park: Combines wildlife viewing with picturesque beaches.

Advanced Trails

- Cerro Chirripó: Costa Rica's highest peak offers a challenging trek with breathtaking views at the summit.
- Corcovado National Park: Multi-day treks through one of the most biodiverse regions on the planet.

Pro Tip: Always pack plenty of water, insect repellent, and sturdy footwear. Guided tours often enhance the experience with local insights.

Water Adventures: Kayaking, Snorkeling, and Fishing

Kayaking

- Paddle through serene mangroves, open seas, or tranquil rivers.
- Best Spots:
  - Golfo Dulce (South Pacific): A biodiversity hotspot with calm waters.
  - Tortuguero Canals (Caribbean Coast): Glide through jungle waterways teeming with wildlife.

Snorkeling

- Costa Rica's marine biodiversity shines beneath the waves.
- Top Spots:
- Caño Island: Clear waters with vibrant coral reefs.
- Playa Conchal (Guanacaste): Calm waters ideal for beginners.

Fishing

- A dream destination for anglers, Costa Rica offers world-class sportfishing.
- Best Locations:
  - Quepos: Renowned for sailfish and marlin.
  - Papagayo Peninsula: Great for tuna and mahi-mahi.

Pro Tip: January to April is peak season for Pacific sailfish.

Relaxation & Wellness: Hot Springs, Spas, and Yoga

Hot Springs

- Costa Rica's volcanic activity creates naturally heated springs perfect for relaxation.
- Top Spots:

- Tabacón (Arenal): Luxurious springs surrounded by lush gardens.
- Río Perdido (Guanacaste): A hidden gem with thermal pools in a canyon.

Pro Tip: Visit in the evening for a magical experience under the stars.

Spas

- Indulge in traditional treatments using natural ingredients like volcanic mud and coffee.
- Top Locations: Papagayo Peninsula, Manuel Antonio, and Arenal.

Yoga Retreats

- Costa Rica is a global yoga haven with retreats combining mindfulness and nature.
- Best Areas:
  - Nicoya Peninsula: Known for wellness and yoga communities.
  - Dominical (South Pacific): Tranquil retreats by the beach.

Costa Rican Culture & Cuisine

In addition to its amazing wildlife and landscapes, Costa Rica is home to some of the greatest cuisine you will ever taste, as well as a rich cultural heritage. Costa Rican culture is characterized by friendliness, simplicity, and the idea of Pura Vida, which sums up the laid-back, upbeat, and contented lifestyle that the people there live. Every encounter, meal, and experience will evoke the spirit of Pura Vida, whether you're dining at a fine dining establishment or exploring a small village.

The Pura Vida Way of Life

"Pura Vida" (translated as "Pure Life") is more than just a saying – it's the heartbeat of Costa Rican culture. It represents living life to the fullest, savoring the present moment, and appreciating the beauty in simplicity. From the friendly "Pura Vida!" Costa Ricans are renowned for their upbeat outlook and strong bond with nature, which contributes to their relaxed approach to both work and life.

- Mindset: Costa Ricans prioritize happiness, family, and well-being over stress or material gain. They are quick to share a smile and offer a "Pura Vida!" in the midst of everyday moments.
- Nature: In a country that is a nature lover's paradise, Pura Vida extends beyond people – it's a way of living in harmony with the environment. Costa Ricans take pride in their biodiversity and sustainable practices.

Festivals, Traditions, and Celebrations

Costa Rica's rich history, religious influences, and reverence for the natural world are all reflected in its colorful festivals, music, and customs.

- Festa de los Diablitos (Boruca): This customary celebration honors the resistance of the indigenous Boruca people against Spanish colonization and is held in December and January. The celebration includes rituals, dances, and vibrant masks.

- One of the most significant religious holidays in Costa Rica is Semana Santa, or Holy Week, which is celebrated with processions, church services, and family get-togethers. It's a time for reflection and spiritual development.

- Carnival de Puntarenas: A vibrant celebration of the area's Afro-Caribbean roots that takes place in February or March and features parades, music, and dances.

- La Feria Internacional del Mar: An annual festival dedicated to the sea, where locals and tourists come together to celebrate the ocean with seafood, music, and marine conservation activities.

Pro Tip: If you visit Costa Rica during a festival, you'll experience the vibrant community spirit, and you'll have a chance to connect with the local culture in a unique and exciting way.

Food Culture: Must-Try Dishes

Made with fresh, local ingredients, Costa Rican cuisine is a delicious blend of Afro-Caribbean, Spanish, and indigenous flavors. The cuisine is straightforward but tasty, with a focus on fresh fruit, rice, and beans. In order to really experience Costa Rican culture, you must sample these foods.

- Casado: The ultimate Costa Rican dish, casado is a hearty meal consisting of rice, beans, plantains, salad, and your choice of protein – usually chicken, beef, or fish. It's served in almost every local restaurant or "soda," offering a true taste of everyday Costa Rican life.

- Gallo Pinto: A traditional breakfast dish made of rice and beans stir-fried together with onions, peppers, and cilantro. Often paired with eggs and tortillas, it's a comforting and energizing way to start the day.

- Ceviche: A refreshing and tangy dish typically made from fresh fish or shrimp marinated in citrus juices (lime and orange), then mixed with onions, cilantro, and peppers. Perfect for a coastal meal after a long day at the beach.

- Olla de Carne: A traditional beef stew made with root vegetables like yam, potato, and carrots. It's slow-cooked to perfection, rich in flavor, and hearty enough to keep you energized on your Costa Rican adventures.

- Tamales: Costa Ricans also enjoy tamales, made of corn dough stuffed with meats or vegetables, wrapped in banana leaves, and steamed. A beloved comfort food often enjoyed during the holidays.

Dining Guide: Local Sodas and Fine Dining

In Costa Rica, eating isn't just about relieving hunger – it's about community, culture, and connection. Whether you're dining in a rustic "soda" (a small local eatery) or at a fine-dining restaurant, the cuisine and environment are guaranteed to be unforgettable.

Local Sodas

These small, family-owned eateries serve the heart and soul of Costa Rican cuisine. The best part? You'll find authentic dishes at unbeatable prices.

- El Soda La Amistad (San José): A charming soda serving traditional casados and hearty Olla de Carne.

- Soda Tapia (San José): One of the most famous sodas in the capital, known for its delicious and affordable Costa Rican meals.

- Soda La Casona (Quepos): Located near Manuel Antonio National Park, this place serves up amazing ceviche and rice dishes with fresh local ingredients.

Fine Dining

More sophisticated dining alternatives that combine regional ingredients with a global flair are available because to Costa Rica's expanding culinary industry. Costa Rican chefs are gaining recognition for their inventiveness in creating modern and fusion food.

- Le Monastère (San José): An elegant restaurant offering gourmet meals in an old monastery, with breathtaking views of the city.
- Café de los Deseos (San José): This is the spot for innovative, farm-to-table dishes showcasing the best of Costa Rican produce.
- Ostra del Mar (Guanacaste): For a fine dining experience on the beach, Ostra del Mar offers fresh seafood and exquisite cocktails while you enjoy the ocean breeze.

Pro Tip: While fine dining is a great way to treat yourself, don't miss out on the "sodas" – they are the true gems where you can taste authentic Costa Rican food in a casual, welcoming setting.

Eco-Tourism in Costa Rica

Costa Rica leads the world in ecotourism, allowing visitors to enjoy its beautiful beaches, lush jungles, and abundant biodiversity while reducing their environmental impact. Because of its unmatched dedication to sustainability and conservation, the nation is a top choice for tourists who care about the environment. Costa Rica has all you need to travel sustainably and take in the natural beauty of the country, whether you're staying in eco-lodges, helping with conservation initiatives, or exploring the untamed landscapes.

Sustainable Travel Tips

For many Costa Ricans, traveling responsibly is a way of life rather than merely a decision. Here are some pointers to help you travel the nation with caution.

- Respect Wildlife: There is an incredible variety of wildlife in Costa Rica, but it is important to preserve their natural habitat. Never feed wild animals, stay on designated pathways, and don't interfere with their natural behavior

- Use Eco-Friendly Transportation: When exploring Costa Rica, choose eco-friendly modes of transportation like bicycles or electric cars, as well as shared trips and public transportation. Car-sharing programs are also available in several cities.

- Lessen Plastic Use: Although Costa Rica has made great progress in cutting down on plastic waste, you can still help by bringing reusable containers, shopping bags, and water bottles.

- Conserve Water and Energy: In many parts of Costa Rica, water is a precious resource. Use water-saving devices, take shorter showers, and switch off lights when not in use.

Pro Tip: When booking tours and activities, ask operators about their sustainability practices to ensure you're supporting companies that prioritize the environment.

Eco-Lodges and Green Hotels

Eco-lodges and green hotels in Costa Rica prioritize sustainability while providing a fully immersed natural experience. These lodgings, which are frequently constructed with eco-friendly materials, run on renewable energy, and dedicated to lessening their environmental effect, blend in perfectly with their surroundings.

- Lipa Rios Lodge (Osa Peninsula): Situated in the center of the Osa Peninsula, one of the world's most biodiverse places, is this opulent eco-lodge. From the utilization of solar energy to the application of water-saving measures, the lodge runs according to the strictest environmental guidelines.

- Monteverde Inn (Monteverde Cloud Forest): This eco-lodge, which is tucked away in Monteverde's cloud forests, provides stunning vistas and a dedication to conservation. Visitors can discover local environmental initiatives while exploring the nearby woodland.

- Selina (Various Locations): Selina provides eco-lodging in a number of large cities and seaside towns and is well-known for its environmentally friendly architecture and community-based philosophy. Zero-waste programs and collaborations with regional conservation groups are examples of their environmental endeavors.

- Tree House Lodge (Caribbean Coast): Enjoy breathtaking views of the jungle and the Caribbean Sea while lodging in distinctive, environmentally friendly treehouses. In order to preserve ecological balance, the lodge places a strong emphasis on conservation and works closely with nearby communities.

Pro Tip: When booking eco-lodges, look for certifications like CERTIFIED SUSTAINABLE TOURISM (CST), which ensures that accommodations meet high environmental standards.

Volunteering Opportunities

For tourists who wish to experience Costa Rica's natural beauty and give back, there are many options available. One of the best ways to experience Costa Rican culture and support social and environmental causes is to volunteer there.

- Wildlife Conservation: To support the preservation of endangered species and their ecosystems, join groups like Osa Conservation or the Costa Rica Wildlife Sanctuary. Volunteers support scientific initiatives, such as the conservation of sea turtles, and animal rescue and rehabilitation.

- Reforestation Programs: Costa Rica is a great destination for tourists looking to participate in reforestation initiatives because of its dedication to sustainability. Volunteers are invited to assist in tree planting and native ecosystem restoration by the Costa Rican National Forestry Office and other regional non-governmental organizations.

- Community Development: Help build homes, provide healthcare, or support local education programs for impoverished communities by volunteering with groups like TECHO Costa Rica or La Fundación Humanitaria de Costa Rica.

- Eco-Tourism Projects: If you have a strong interest in eco-tourism, you might want to volunteer with wildlife reserves, eco-lodges, or local guides to assist spread awareness of conservation initiatives and encourage sustainable travel.

Pro Tip: Many eco-lodges and tour companies in Costa Rica offer volunteering packages where you can combine your stay with hands-on conservation work.

Supporting Local Communities

It's crucial to have a positive influence on the local community while in Costa Rica. Supporting regional companies, craftspeople, and projects makes sure that tourism helps the nation's citizens and encourages environmentally friendly behavior.

- Encourage Indigenous Communities: Numerous indigenous communities, each with their own traditions and rituals, call Costa Rica home. To support local artists and guarantee just remuneration, buy handcrafted items like textiles, pottery, and beadwork straight from them.

- Shop Local: Rather than going to big-box stores, get items, food, and souvenirs from neighborhood markets. Locally produced goods abound at San José's Central Market and tiny rural markets, offering anything from handcrafted jewelry and artwork to fresh fruits and vegetables.

- Eco-Friendly Tours: Choose small, regionally run tour companies that back conservation and education initiatives rooted in the community. This guarantees that the communities that are hosting you directly benefit from tourism.

- Take Part in Community Projects: Sustainable tourism provides funding for local projects in several Costa Rican municipalities. There are countless ways to give back to the community while you're there, from taking part in conservation education seminars to assisting with beach clean-ups.

Pro Tip: Look for companies that value fair trade, ethical sourcing, and environmental sustainability, and always inquire about how your purchases are helping the community.

Tailored Itineraries

Whether you're looking to take a short vacation or fully immerse yourself in the country's breathtaking landscapes and culture, Costa Rica has something to offer everyone. With the following customized itineraries, we've made it simple for you to plan your ideal Costa Rican vacation, highlighting must-see locations, exciting days, and leisurely moments that perfectly capture the essence of Costa Rica. All of these itineraries are based on the most recent travel trends and insider knowledge to ensure that your trip is one to remember.

3-Day Getaway: Highlights of Costa Rica

This 3-day plan is ideal if you're pressed for time but yet want to see the best parts of Costa Rica. You'll depart with a genuine sense of what makes Costa Rica so unique, full of adventure, wildlife, and culture.

Day 1: Central Valley and San José

- Morning: Get to the capital of Costa Rica, San José. Visit the National Museum of Costa Rica first thing in the morning. Housed in a historic building, the museum features exhibits that provide information about the history and biodiversity of the nation.

- In the afternoon, take a tour of La Sabana Park, the city's green center, and stop by Mercado Central for a traditional rice and bean lunch known as gallo pinto.

- Evening: Take a short drive to Poás Volcano National Park for a quick visit to one of the most active volcanoes in the country. If time permits, enjoy dinner at a local restaurant and experience the nightlife in downtown San José.

Day 2: La Fortuna and Arenal

- Morning: Travel to Arenal Volcano by car (about three hours). Take a guided hike through the lush rainforest and lava fields of the Arenal Volcano National Park to start your day.

- Afternoon: Unwind at the volcano's natural hot springs after your hike. Tabacón Hot Springs is a well-liked location where you may soak in thermal pools encircled by tropical plants.

- Evening: Savor a picturesque meal while taking in the volcano's vistas and the setting sun.

Manuel Antonio National Park on Day Three

- In the morning, travel three hours from Arenal to Manuel Antonio National Park. Hike along rainforest-surrounded pathways in the morning while taking in the park's breathtaking beaches and fauna.

- Afternoon: Lounge on the white sandy beaches, swim in the turquoise waters, and enjoy the peaceful environment of the park.
- Evening: End your day with a beachfront dinner in the nearby town of Quepos before heading back to San José.

7-Day Adventure: Volcanoes, Beaches, and Forests

You can explore Costa Rica's many ecosystems, from serene beaches to active volcanoes, in greater detail over a week there. This seven-day schedule will keep you occupied with wildlife encounters, culture, and adventure.

Arrival in San José on Day 1

- Morning: Arrive and settle in.
- Afternoon: Become acquainted with San José's museums, marketplaces, and local attractions by going on a guided city tour.
- Evening: Visit Restaurante Grano de Oro for a traditional   Costa   Rican   meal.

Day 2: La Fortuna and the Arenal Volcano

- Good morning: Morning: Drive to La Fortuna for three hours. For breathtaking views of the volcano and the surrounding vegetation, hike in Arenal Volcano National Park.

- Afternoon: Visit La Fortuna Waterfall, one of the most beautiful waterfalls in Costa Rica. Afterward, enjoy the hot springs and a relaxing evening in town.

Day 3: Monteverde Cloud Forest

- Morning: Drive to Monteverde (approximately 3 hours). Begin your day with a guided tour through the Monteverde Cloud Forest Reserve, known for its rich biodiversity and canopy tours.

- Afternoon: Visit the Monteverde Butterfly Gardens or try a night walk tour to see the nocturnal wildlife.

- Evening: Dinner at a local restaurant with views of the forest.

Day 4: Manuel Antonio National Park

- **Morning:** Drive to Manuel Antonio (about 3 hours). Start your day at the park with a guided nature walk to spot monkeys, sloths, and tropical birds.

- **Afternoon:** Relax on the pristine beaches of Playa Espadilla or go for a swim in the crystal-clear water.

- **Evening:** Enjoy the laid-back atmosphere and beachside dining at one of the restaurants in the area.

Day 5: South Pacific – Osa Peninsula

- **Morning:** Head south to the Osa Peninsula (about 3.5 hours), one of the most biodiverse regions in the world.

- **Afternoon:** Visit Corcovado National Park, known for its rich wildlife, including jaguars, tapirs, and scarlet macaws. You can also go on a boat tour in Golfo Dulce to spot dolphins and whales.

- Evening: Stay in a remote eco-lodge to immerse yourself in the region's natural beauty.

Day 6: Puerto Viejo – Caribbean Coast

- Morning: Travel to Puerto Viejo (about 4 hours). Relax on the laid-back beaches and experience the Afro-Caribbean culture of this coastal town.
- Afternoon: Visit the Jaguar Rescue Center or enjoy a guided tour through the nearby Cahuita National Park, famous for its wildlife and coral reefs.
- Evening: Try local Caribbean dishes like rice and beans with coconut milk.

Day 7: Return to San José

- Morning: Head back to San José (about 4.5 hours) for your final day.

- Afternoon: Last-minute shopping or a visit to the Pre-Columbian Gold Museum to round out your Costa Rican adventure.
- Evening: Enjoy a farewell dinner at La Esquina de Buenos Aires, a cozy Argentinian restaurant in the heart of San José.

14-Day Immersion: The Ultimate Costa Rica Experience

A 14-day itinerary gives you the opportunity to thoroughly discover Costa Rica's many ecosystems and cultural treasures, making it the ideal choice for those seeking the most extensive Costa Rican journey. A genuine immersion in Costa Rican culture and natural beauties is guaranteed as you travel through volcanic mountains, tropical rainforests, lively coastal towns, and undiscovered treasures.

Days 1-3: San José and Central Valley

- Explore the capital city and its nearby attractions like Poás Volcano and La Paz Waterfall

Gardens. Visit local coffee plantations for a full cultural immersion.

Days 4-5: Arenal and La Fortuna

- Take a hike on the Arenal Volcano and unwind in the thermal springs. . Don't miss La Fortuna Waterfall and an adventure-filled day of ziplining or horseback riding through the rainforest.

Days 6-7: Monteverde

- Discover the cloud forests, enjoy canopy tours, and experience the wildlife in this biodiverse region. Visit Monteverde's Butterfly Gardens and go on a guided night walk.

Days 8-9: Manuel Antonio

- Enjoy beaches, wildlife spotting, and adventure activities like surfing or kayaking. Take a guided tour of Manuel Antonio National Park and relax in the laid-back coastal town.

Days 10-11: Osa Peninsula

- Venture into Corcovado National Park for a once-in-a-lifetime wildlife experience. Stay in eco-lodges and participate in conservation efforts. Participate in conservation initiatives while lodging in eco-lodges.

Days 12-13: Puerto Viejo & Cahuita National Park

- Experience the Caribbean's Afro-Caribbean culture, vibrant beaches, and eco-tourism. Visit Cahuita for snorkeling or hiking through its jungle trails.

Day 14: Return to San José

- Spend your final day shopping, visiting museums, or just relaxing before heading home.

```````
```````

Practical Tips for Travelers

Costa Rica is a friendly place that offers a mix of leisure, adventure, and a lively culture. Here are some crucial, doable suggestions to aid simplify and enhance your trip, guaranteeing a pleasant and unforgettable trip across this stunning nation.

Money Matters: Currency, ATMs, and Tipping Culture

Currency

The official currency of Costa Rica is the colón (CRC). Although U.S. dollars are often accepted, particularly in tourist destinations, it's a good idea to keep extra cash on hand for little purchases or when traveling to more rural areas. Although the exchange rate is subject to fluctuations, 1 USD will be approximately 550 CRC in 2025.

ATM

Major cities like San José, La Fortuna, and Guanacaste are replete with ATMs. It's crucial to verify the machine's settings, but the majority of ATMs can dispense both colones and US dollars. Since not all places have ATMs, exercise caution when taking out cash in isolated areas. Using a credit card that has no overseas transaction fees can also be a more affordable choice because some banks impose an international fee.

Credit and Debit Cards

Visa and Mastercard are the most widely accepted credit cards, especially in touristy areas, hotels, and restaurants. American Express is less commonly accepted, and smaller businesses may not take cards, so carrying cash is always a good idea.

Tipping Culture

Tipping is appreciated in Costa Rica, but it's not mandatory. Here are some guidelines:

- Restaurants: A 10% service charge is often included in the bill. If not, a tip of 10-15% is common.
- Taxis: Add a little gratuity or round up the fare.
- Drivers and Guides: A generous tip is 10–20% of the trip price.
- Hotel Staff: A small tip of around 1,000 CRC per day for housekeepers is appreciated.

Language Tips: Essential Spanish Phrases

Spanish is the official language of Costa Rica, though English is widely spoken in tourist areas. However, learning a few basic phrases can enhance your experience and connect you more deeply with the local culture. To help you began, consider these essential phrases:

- Pura Vida! – The Costa Rican expression of happiness, meaning "pure life" or "good vibes."
- Hola, ¿cómo estás? – Hi, how are you?
- Gracias – Thank you.
- Por favor – Please.
- ¿Cuánto cuesta? – How much does it cost?
- ¿Dónde está el baño? – Where is the bathroom?
- Habla inglés? – Do you speak English?
- Una cerveza, por favor – A beer, please.
- ¡Adiós! – Goodbye!

Even if you don't become fluent, locals will appreciate your efforts to speak Spanish, and it will enrich your travel experience.

Costa Rican Weather: Regional Breakdown

Despite having a tropical climate, Costa Rica's topography produces a range of weather patterns depending on your location. Planning your activities and packing appropriately will be made easier if you are aware of the weather in various areas.

Central Valley (San José, Alajuela, Heredia)

- Weather: Generally mild, with average temperatures around 70-80°F (21-27°C) year-round.
- Best Time to Visit: Dry season from December to April for pleasant weather, though you can visit year-round.

Pacific Coast (Guanacaste, Nicoya Peninsula, Manuel Antonio)

- Weather: Hot and dry during the dry season (December-April), while the rainy season (May-

November) brings afternoon showers. Temperatures range from 80-95°F (27-35°C).

- Best Time to Visit: Dry season is ideal for beach vacations.

Caribbean Coast (Puerto Viejo, Tortuguero)

- Weather: More rainfall than the Pacific side, but temperatures are consistently warm (80-85°F/27-29°C). November through April is the dry season, and May through October is the wet season.

- Best Time to Visit: November to April, when rainfall is lower.

Northern Highlands (Arenal, Monteverde)

- Weather: Temperatures are cooler and can range from 60-75°F (15-24°C) due to the higher altitude. Expect rain year-round, but especially during the green season (May-November).

- Best Time to Visit: Dry season for clearer skies and better hiking conditions.

Osa Peninsula (Corcovado)

- Weather: Hot and humid, with consistent rainfall throughout the year. Temperatures can be 85-90°F (29-32°C).
- Best Time to Visit: December to April, when the weather is drier, though it remains humid.

Travel Apps and Tools

Costa Rica is a traveler-friendly country, but having the right tools can make your trip even smoother. Here are some essential apps and online tools to help with navigation, bookings, and local experiences:

Google Maps

- Navigate Costa Rica's roads, find restaurants, hotels, and top destinations with ease. The app also works offline if you download maps ahead of time.

Waze

- Particularly useful for navigating local traffic in cities like San José. It gives real-time updates on road conditions, accidents, and traffic jams.

TripAdvisor

- For finding the best-rated restaurants, hotels, tours, and activities based on real traveler reviews.

Costa Rica Travel Guide App

- A comprehensive guide to attractions, national parks, wildlife, and more. It also includes practical tips and a currency converter.

WhatsApp

- Widely used for communication in Costa Rica, whether with tour operators, hotels, or fellow travelers.

XE Currency Converter

- Helps you track exchange rates and convert between U.S. dollars and Costa Rican colóns.

Airbnb

- For booking unique stays, from beach-front homes to jungle eco-lodges, especially in areas outside of major cities.

Uber

- Available in major cities like San José and some beach towns, Uber provides an affordable and convenient alternative to taxis.

Resources & Contacts

Even though Costa Rica is a friendly and safe place to visit, it's a good idea to have emergency contacts on hand in case something unforeseen occurs. The following is a list of crucial numbers to have on hand when traveling:

- Emergency Services (Ambulance, Fire, Police): 911
- Tourism Police (Policía Turística): +506 2295-2335
- Medical Emergency (Red Cross): +506 128-3800
- National Animal Rescue: +506 2560-3031
- Poison Control: +506 2222-7315
- Tourist Information: +506 2258-4924

Note: Costa Rica's emergency services are generally efficient, but it's recommended to have your hotel or accommodations' contact information and address on hand, as this can assist emergency services in finding you more quickly.

Recommended Tour Operators

Costa Rica is a treasure trove of natural wonders, and to make the most out of your trip, it's often best to book through a reputable tour operator. Here are some of the most trusted and highly recommended ones that offer exceptional tours, experiences, and personalized itineraries:

Costa Rica Expeditions

Website: www.costaricaexpeditions.com

Known for luxury travel and expertly curated tours, Costa Rica Expeditions offers tailored adventures, wildlife excursions, and eco-friendly trips throughout the country.

Tropical Adventures

Website: www.tropicaladventures.com

Tropical Adventures provides fun-packed trips ranging from zip-lining to wildlife safaris and bird-watching. They're a great choice for both adrenaline junkies and those seeking relaxation in nature.

Wave Riders Surf School

Website: www.waveriderscr.com

Located in Guanacaste, Wave Riders offers surf lessons for all levels of surfers, from beginners to advanced. They also provide surf trips to some of Costa Rica's best beaches.

Monteverde Wild

Website: www.monteverdewild.com

Monteverde Wild offers specialized tours around the Monteverde Cloud Forest Reserve, emphasizing sustainability and conservation. Great for eco-tourists and nature lovers.

Arenal Mundo Aventura

Website: www.arenalmundoaventura.com

Arenal Mundo Aventura provides thrilling zip-lining and waterfall tours, as well as an opportunity to explore the famous Arenal Volcano. A great choice for adventure seekers.

Tortuguero Tours

Website: www.tortuguerotours.com

Specializing in tours around the Tortuguero National Park, this operator offers boat tours through the park's intricate canal systems, as well as turtle-watching during nesting season.

Where to Book Activities and Excursions

Booking activities and excursions in Costa Rica is easy and can be done through a variety of trusted platforms and local operators. Here are a few great places to book your adventures:

Viator

Website: www.viator.com

Viator is an excellent platform for booking tours and activities across Costa Rica. You'll find an extensive selection of day trips, nature tours, wildlife excursions, and cultural experiences.

GetYourGuide

Website: www.getyourguide.com

A well-known international booking platform that offers hundreds of Costa Rican experiences, from guided hikes to kayaking tours, to zip-lining adventures.

Klook

Website: www.klook.com

Klook is a great resource for travelers seeking exclusive deals on activities like visiting Arenal Volcano, Monteverde Cloud Forest, or taking a boat tour through Tortuguero.

Costa Rica Local Tours

Website: www.costaricalocaltours.com

For those who prefer booking directly with local operators, Costa Rica Local Tours offers a broad selection of eco-tours, adventure activities, and family-friendly experiences in major tourist destinations.

Airbnb Experiences

Website: www.airbnb.com

For more personalized and off-the-beaten-path excursions, check out Airbnb Experiences. You can book everything from cooking classes to surf lessons, guided hikes, and cultural tours.

Final Tips for a Memorable Trip

In Costa Rica, adventure, culture, and environment all combine to produce once-in-a-lifetime experience. Here are some last-minute suggestions to make your time in this stunning nation as seamless and pleasurable as possible as you finalize your preparations.

Staying Connected: Wi-Fi and SIM Cards

Staying connected is crucial in today's society, whether it's for communication, map navigation, or photo sharing with loved ones. What you should know is as follows:

- Wi-Fi: Most Costa Rican hotels, hostels, and restaurants offer free Wi-Fi, especially in large towns and popular tourist destinations. Signal strength, however, can differ, particularly in national parks or rural locations. When making reservations for lodging, it's wise to confirm availability.

- SIM Cards: Think about getting a local SIM card so you can stay connected during your journey. SIM cards for major providers including Claro, Movistar, and Kolbi are available at the airport and in local shops. These companies provide traveler-friendly prepaid plans with data bundles. One economical way to avoid expensive roaming charges from foreign providers is to use a local SIM card.

- Mobile Hotspots: Renting a portable Wi-Fi hotspot is a fantastic choice if you require more dependable internet for work or intend to utilize several devices. These can be reserved in advance online or at airports.

Cultural Etiquette and Do's & Don'ts

Costa Rica is known for its friendly and warm-hearted people. Still, it's always good to be mindful of cultural norms. Here are a few dos and don'ts to keep in mind:

Do's

- Respect Local Customs: Costa Ricans are proud of their heritage and culture, and they appreciate travelers who show respect. Always greet with a smile and say "¡Pura Vida!" (The Costa Rican slogan, "pure life," which embodies a carefree and optimistic outlook on life).

- Use "Tico" and "Tica": Locals often refer to themselves as Ticos (men) and Ticas (women), and it's a term of endearment and pride. Using it in casual conversations can make you seem more friendly and connected.

- Dress Modestly: While Costa Rica is a tropical paradise, modest dress is appreciated in local communities, especially in rural areas. In cities and at the beach, more relaxed clothing is acceptable.

- **Be Patient:** Costa Ricans value a slower pace of life. "Tranquilo" (calm down) is a phrase you might hear often, and it's a reflection of their easygoing nature Relax and embrace the "Pura Vida" lifestyle!

Don'ts

- **Don't Rush:** Costa Ricans aren't typically in a rush, so if things seem a bit slow, don't get frustrated. Enjoy the relaxed pace and let the good vibes come naturally.

- **Don't Point:** Pointing at people, especially in a public space, is considered impolite. Instead, make gestures with your entire hand.

- **Don't Expect to Bargain Everywhere:** While bargaining is common in local markets, it's not a universal practice in Costa Rica, especially in more formal retail settings or established businesses. Be sure to assess the situation before attempting to negotiate a price.

- Don't Tip Too Little: Tipping is customary in Costa Rica, especially in the tourism industry. A tip of ten to fifteen percent is customarily appreciated in restaurants. Also, tour guides, drivers, and hotel staff will expect tips for good service.

Getting the Most Out of Your Costa Rican Vacation

With countless chances to engage with nature, explore local culture, and create lifelong memories, Costa Rica is an adventure playground. Take into account the following if you want to get the most out of your stay here:

- Plan a Balance of Activities: While Costa Rica's natural beauty is undeniably its main draw, don't forget to take time to enjoy the country's culture, beaches, and wildlife. A combination of outdoor adventures, relaxing downtime, and cultural exploration will ensure you experience the full spectrum of what this amazing country has to offer.

- Don't Over-Schedule: Costa Rica's attractions are spread out across the country, and travel times can vary depending on road conditions. It's better to choose fewer destinations and enjoy them fully rather than rush between them. After all, it's about quality experiences, not quantity.

- Respect Nature: Costa Rica's biodiversity is one of the most impressive in the world, and conservation efforts are a big part of the country's identity. Be mindful of your impact on the environment by respecting wildlife, following park regulations, and leaving no trace.

- Engage with Locals: The heart of Costa Rica lies in its people. Take the time to chat with locals, learn about their way of life, and try your hand at tico cuisine or participating in a local festival. Costa Ricans are known for being friendly and will make you feel at home.

- Embrace the "Pura Vida" Lifestyle: Most importantly, let go of the stress and embrace the joy of the moment. Costa Rica's laid-back atmosphere invites you to appreciate life's simpler pleasures. Whether you're watching the sunset over the Pacific or hiking to a hidden waterfall, immerse yourself in the "Pura Vida" experience—it's not just a phrase, it's a way of life.

Index

Made in the USA
Monee, IL
27 January 2025